THE INTERVIEW AT WORK

John Fletcher

Duckworth

First published in 1973 by
Gerald Duckworth & Co. Ltd.
The Old Piano Factory
43 Gloucester Crescent, London NW1

A /658.31

ISBN 0 7156 0727 8
ISBN 0 7156 0728 6

Printed in Great Britain by
Unwin Brothers Limited, Old Woking
Typesetting by
Specialised Offset Services Limited,Liverpool

THE INTERVIEW AT WORK

Contents

Preface

Preface

There are long books about interviewing, particularly interviewing for recruitment, and there are chapters about interviewing in books on other subjects. This book is meant to fill the gap between the two.

It is based on eight years' experience of running courses in interviewing for industry and the Civil Service. It should therefore be of practical value to the manager and administrator. My hope is that it is not just more background reading for managers, but that it will serve the manager faced with a difficult interview, if he reads the appropriate part of the book and checks through the notes. The book is also intended for students taking professional examinations in Communication, and for those teaching the subject. The role-plays at the end presuppose classroom study; they are written for post-experience students on in-Company courses, but with a few amendments to the roles, all can play.

Some people object to the idea that interviews can be divided up into grievance, instruction, correction, and so forth. They point out that real interviews often cut across these arbitrary dividing lines. Well, sometimes they do and sometimes they don't, and sometimes they do because there is a muddle. But it seems to me that there is a lot to be said for looking at different kinds of interviews separately, even if the separation is theoretical. A man is more likely to be able to steer a car and change gear simultaneously if, when he was learning, he practised steering in one lesson and changing gear in another.

Many of the individuals and organizations with whom I have worked will recognize some contribution of their own. I thank them all, though I cannot name them all, for the ideas and help they have given. I should like specifically to acknowledge the guidance of Tom Fassam, who was the ideal teacher. When he was my boss, he used to say of some operation: 'If it goes well, you take the credit; if it goes badly, the blame is mine.' (If all managers followed his example, instead of doing the opposite, how different the world would be.) Now I can return the compliment. If anything in the book is creditable, the credit is probably due to him. For its faults I alone am to blame.

Chapter One Principles of Interviewing

1 DEFINITION OF 'INTERVIEW'

An interview is a meeting of two people, face to face, to accomplish a known purpose by discussion.

This is the definition implied in this book, except for a short look into the panel selection interview, which involves more than two people.

In most of the interviews discussed the two people are a subordinate and his boss. We are concerned with the interview 'at work', but no doubt the principles apply elsewhere.

If you remove from this definition all reference to a purpose, what is left defines a conversation. A conversation with a purpose, a known purpose, becomes an interview. These definitions are not just games with words; the fact is that interviews can become conversations if the purpose is forgotten.

Much of the awe that surrounds the interview would disappear if it were called a purposeful conversation. Human beings converse merrily from an early age, and develop skills in conversing. They discover what amuses and what does not. They learn how to recognise the non-verbal signals in a conversation, and how to handle difficult people and difficult subjects. All this is valuable preparation for interviewing. True, some people are not 'good conversationalists'; usually this means that they cannot readily think of things to say. This should be no problem to an interviewer, because the known purpose fixes the subject. If there is nothing more to be said to the purpose, the interview should end.

Some of the unjustified assumptions made about interviews would also disappear. People have purposeful conversations on buses, in a workshop, on their way to or from the canteen, but tend to think of an interview as something that must be in an office. But the good interviewer asks himself where the best place is, and considers some alternatives to the office. A car, a pub, a park may be more successful.

The word 'formal' comes in here. It is often used to categorize interviews, but unfortunately it is ambiguous, and in discussing the interview, this leads to misunderstanding. A formal interview may be

1 an interview with a purpose and a plan;
2 an interview held by appointment and at an agreed place;
3 an interview of which a written record is kept, as with a
  'formal reprimand'.

There are doubtless other meanings in the phrase 'a formal interview'. It is not much use unless those who use the phrase also say which kind of 'formal' they mean. All the interviews we are concerned with now are formal in sense 1, as they have a purpose by definition and a plan to achieve the purpose. They are not necessarily formal in sense 2, and only the exceptional cases will be formal in sense 3.

2 *SUMMARY NOTES*

Aims

1 To improve the performance of the boss, the subordinate,
  or the organization generally
2 To test or improve morale, attitudes and feelings
3 To get information

4 To give information
5 To enable the subordinate (not the boss) to let off steam, or get something off his chest
6 To analyse a situation, solve a problem, or specify recommendations
7 To implement the policy of senior management
8 To remove difficulties or clear up misunderstandings
9 To check how successful a previous interview was

Preparation

Preparation is necessary, even if it has to be done by thinking quickly during the first few minutes of the interview.

1 Clear your mind about the purposes of the interview

Do not try and do something which would be better done in some other way, such as a large meeting or a circular
Do not set your self a purpose which you cannot achieve in the time
Do not try to do a job which is really someone else's

2 Study the subject or subjects

Get necessary information or facts
Issue advance information if necessary
Note the main issues to be dealt with
Anticipate probable conflicts of opinion, interest or value

3 Estimate how long the interview will last

4 Outline a plan for the discussion

Think out the opening statement
Consider opening questions
Plan intermediate phases, with timings if necessary

Build up a picture of the final summary, with conclusions
and action if necessary, but be prepared to modify these as
the interview proceeds
If 'problem-solving', consider the alternative solutions which
may be proposed
Make notes of the plan, to refer to in the interview

5 Have everything ready

Choose a suitable place
Ensure privacy and eliminate distractions
Prepare supporting documents, pen, and paper
Give adequate warning if appropriate

3   *Structure*

1 Introduce the subject, or subjects

State the topic in a few words
Indicate the time available for consideration
Provide the essential information:
    Background
    Facts
    Main points
Clarify the purpose and scope of the interview:
    Friendly
    Official
    Confidential to whom
Outline the sequence of the interview (a 'logical pathway')
Open the discussion with a carefully framed question

2   Guide the discussion

Adjust the degree and nature of control to the needs of the
changing situation

4

Draw out information, facts, experience, opinions and suggestions
Distinguish and assemble these in an orderly arrangement
Restate them in your own words
Ensure that the interviewee understands and accepts your restatement
Clear up misunderstandings
Keep discussion on the subject, without intimidating the interviewee
Break up 'circular' sequences and retreading of old ground
Distinguish facts from opinions and inferences
Separate feeling from reasoning
Discourage personal remarks or arguments, usually by ignoring them
Encourage the interviewee to talk
Make full use of stimulating questions
Keep an eye on the time, but as unobtrusively as possible

3 Clarify and crystallize progress

Summarize each phase of the interview
State intermediate conclusions
Clarify points of agreement and disagreement
Check that summaries are understood and agreed

4 Establish results of interview

Give final summary
State what has been agreed, and what must still be resolved
Say if further interview is needed, and when
State conclusions
State action to be taken, if any
Check that these are understood and accepted

Ask how you will discover whether the interview was
successful
Check the aims set for the interview with the actual
consequences
If the interview was not entirely successsful, ask yourself
whether this is for reasons outside the interview. If not, how
could the interview have been more successful? Where did
you go wrong?

3   *STATUS*

The rights and obligations of people are recognisable before
the interview begins. They should be maintained throughout
the interview, and should not (except in an obvious case like
promotion) be affected by the interview.

The smooth conduct of interviews depends on the rights and
obligations given by the organization: in other words, it
depends on the status of the participants. Work cannot be
done efficiently if it is not clear who is responsible for what,
or who is responsible to whom for what. Relationships arise
out of responsibility.

Attempts to undermine the allocation of responsibility defeat
the purpose of the interview. A boss who begins, 'Of course, I
know it's all nonsense, but senior management have said they
want this job done' will forfeit the respect of his subordinate,
will create the feeling that 'if the boss has so little loyalty to
his seniors, he cannot expect me to be loyal to him', and the
job will probably be badly done; the subordinate knows the
boss does not think it is worth doing, and if senior managers
object, it is the boss who will be answerable, not the
subordinate. Delegation is admirable and necessary but it

does not diminish the authority or responsibility of the boss over the subordinate, or the ultimate responsibility of the boss for the actions of his staff.

Status gives security; it establishes where people stand. This may be why interviews are more difficult in large impersonal organisations, with a continuous change of staff, than in a small family firm, where there is always a starting point for the interview in the clear roles and status of those concerned. Status is the framework of decisions, and the drive behind the carrying-out of decisions.

4 TRUTH AND SINCERITY

The idea of a manager's social responsibility is gaining ground. Problems of the environment, of honesty in advertising, of discrimination in employment, are all part of a manager's worries. It is not just pious opinion which says this, nor even public opinion; managers themselves find that their most difficult problems are those involving moral or ethical matters. It is not a case of having to choose between the selfish course and the honest one. Often it is a conflict of loyalties; the manager has to choose between loyalty to one group (say his superior, or his customers) and loyalty to another group (say his subordinates, or other managers, or shareholders, or the nation).

In the interview, one of the main problems is truth. No one listens seriously to an untrustworthy source of information. Therefore, if interviews are to function properly, those holding them must build up a reputation of trust.

Generally the conflict will be between the immediate interests of senior managers, and their long-term interest, or the long-term interest of the 'management profession'. It is easier to refuse a man promotion, or a change of job, if you think his health will not be up to it and you send him for a medical examination. But it is not sincere, if you are not prepared to give him the job when he is cleared; unless you tell him before he goes that the job will not necessarily be his, even if he gets a clean bill of health.

If you are keen to recruit an applicant, it is easy to give him, vaguely, the impression that if he keeps out of trouble he can reach the top.

The most compelling argument against the short-sighted deception is to have to hold the mopping-up interview afterwards.

On a wider scale, a manager may feel obliged, in the interests of his shareholders, and his existing employees, to deny a rumour of redundancy. If this obligation is felt by managers to be one which always overrides the truth, then there ceases to be any point in giving the assurance. A denial is expected, whatever is to happen. It is no more trusted than a statesman is who says that he will not devalue his currency. If all managers put their priorities in this order, the whole profession of management gets a bad reputation, and all suffer. The sad state of industrial relations is in part the result of this kind of mistrust.

The aim of an interview must be legitimate. It is not a legitimate aim (but it may be a legitimate means) to 'take someone down a peg'. It must be a fair balance of conflicting loyalties. If both parties to an interview can only implement policy, it is flattering, but in the long run frustrating, to pretend that the interview can create policy out of nothing.

5 COMMUNICATION WITHOUT WORDS

Interviewers should appreciate the variety and value of non-verbal messages.

1 If not words, then what?

Silence
Pauses, hesitations, 'er's
Tone (upset or relaxed)
Pitch (soprano or bass)
Volume (loud or soft)
Speed
Grunts
Facial expression (eyes are most effective communicators, in relation to the effort involved)
Head (nods) and hands (gestures)
Position (distance, angle of stance, behind a barrier)
Touch
Behaviour (offering a cigarette)
Appearance (dress; tidyness)

2 To convey what sort of message?

Conflict, worry and doubt ('I'm not sure of my facts')
Emotions (fear, anger, pleasure, embarrassment)
Attitudes (admiration, affection, dislike, impatience, loss of confidence, respect, surprise, etc.)
Humour (amusement, cheerfulness)
Habits (personality, class, 'image')
Appeals and threats
'You speak now'

3 Friendliness cues and control cues

In a meeting, many non-verbal cues can be analysed in two ways:

a indicating friendliness or warmth (or a desire for these), and the opposite, hostility

b indicating control and domination (or a bid for these) and the opposite, submissiveness

The cues for friendliness are proximity, the angle formed between two people talking, smiles, eyes, tone of voice and sympathetic grunts.

The cues for control are talking loud, fast, and most of the time, in a confident manner, interrupting, controlling the topic, giving orders, ignoring feedback and relaxation.

Both these systems provide a framework for appeal and threat, reward and punishment, as ways of inducing 'the other to do our will'.

Friendliness and sympathy are rewards. Disagreement and frowns are punishments. The one exercising control can use his power to threaten or reward the submissive. The submissive can appeal to the other's superior power, where the satisfaction of granting the appeal is a reward, and the confession of failure implied by a refusal is distasteful.

4 Examples

The sample interviews on pages 19 to 25 illustrate, as far as a script can, many of these non-verbal exchanges.

6   *KEEPING CONTROL OF THE INTERVIEW*

The interviewer must adapt his ways of controlling discussion
to the situation or phase of the interview (giving or getting
information, solving a problem, or influencing attitudes). The
chief variations in control are to be found in:

a the relative amount of talking done by each party
b the tempo of the interview
c the degree of freedom allowed to the interviewee
d the degree to which digressions are allowed
e the emotional tension or relaxation

For example, in the attitude-influencing situation, the
interviewer will generally do well to control the interview
with a light hand and a loose rein by indirect methods, such
as intermediate and final summaries, and the use of
·questions. He should realize that the most effective influence
on attitudes and opinions will: .

a come from the interviewee stating the problem in his own
   words
b come from allowing him to overstate his case, and so see
   the weaknesses for himself

rather than from trying to ram down views. The interviewer
should maintain an impartial attitude — although he must (if
and when appropriate) sincerely state his own views in an
unprovocative and undogmatic manner.

7 USE OF QUESTIONS

The chief tool of the interviewer is the question. The person asking the questions controls the interview, and so the interviewee should be checked from asking questions except at a stage in the interview set aside by the interviewer for the purpose.

Questions may be used:

1 to encourage the interviewee to relax or to concentrate
2 to draw out knowledge, experience, information, opinion
3 to amplify and explain statements
4 to keep the discussion relevant
5 to bring out distinctions and similarities
6 to re-introduce a point overlooked
7 to encourage intelligent judgment
8 to exercise discipline
9 to check emotional thinking

Questions should seldom be formed in a way which implies criticism or disagreement by the interviewer; such will not serve the purpose of the interview. Thus 'Do you mean . . . or . . .?' should only be used if the interviewer has a genuine and explicable doubt; otherwise 'If I understand you correctly, you are saying . . .' is better.

Questions are 'open' if the length as well as the nature of the answer depends on the answerer, e.g. 'what would be the good and bad results of . . .?' They help the interviewer to assess the mood and personality of the interviewee, as well as obtain information.

'Limiting' questions, or questions which are not open, are capable of being answered 'Yes' or 'No' or very briefly, with little scope for the answerer to influence the answer he gives.

They are useful when the interviewer wants to avoid hesitancy or strain, as when starting an interview with someone shy; or for emphasising a vital point; or bringing an interview back on to the rails.

Who?
Where?   introduce limiting questions
When?

Why?
How?   introduce open questions
What?

8   DIFFICULT PEOPLE AND TOPICS

Interviewees may be

a over-talkative
b irrelevant
c impatient (wanting to jump to a decision)
d closed minds — a single point of view
e dogmatic — making unsupported statements
f duellers — more concerned with winning an argument than finding the best solution to the problem
g destructive and unco-operative
h inattentive; interrupting; or just not listening

In dealing with such people the interviewer should when possible de-personalize the issue away from himself, often by the use of questions which refer the interviewee back to the main objective:

'Do you feel we are making progress . . .?'
'Shall we agree to leave that point for the time being?'
'How does this point of view help us to reach a solution?'

Sometimes a restatement of the topic will bring an interview back on to the rails. In extreme cases an adjournment may be necessary.

Among difficult topics are points involving;

a criticism of higher authority
b comparisons unfavourable to the Company
c disclosure of situations reflecting badly on the employee
d value-judgments of individuals or functions
e new practices which are contrary to a man's pet ideas

The interviewer can agree to investigate a grievance against higher authority; but if he takes sides with the interviewee against higher authority, he changes the relationship with the interviewee, his own status, and the objective of the interview. Embarrassing or emotionally-loaded comments should be drained of their emotional content, and discussion confined to those aspects which the interview can influence and improve.

If the interviewer is careful to remain impartial, objective, unemotional, and sincere, and if he keeps in view the ultimate aims of the meeting, these situations can usually be resolved.

9   *CONTROLLING THE LEVEL OF ANXIETY*

Anxious men are inhibited, and therefore cannot communicate effectively.

BUT: Over-confident, over-relaxed men see no reason to discuss unpleasant matters; they have no motive for doing so; so they do not communicate effectively either.

SO: If the anxiety-level is too high, it should be lowered, and if it is too low, it should be increased.

To *reduce* anxiety

Convey:
    Desire for him to talk
    Trust
    Undivided attention
    No hurry

By:
    Signs of affection/understanding
    Reassurances
    Relaxed conversation
    Relaxing oneself
    Distractions, digressions
    The Grunt Sympathetic
    Offering suggestions, taking care not to arouse resentment;
    non-words are better than words
    Referring indirectly and metaphorically
    Waiting for *him* to have the insight

To *increase* anxiety

Convey:
    Serious nature of subject
    Importance of the occasion
    Authority of communicator
    Urgency
    Formal, cold relationships
    Unpleasant consequences

By the opposite techniques to those for reducing anxiety, and especially:
    Emotional withdrawal

Increasing distance, literally
Precise use of words

And if need be:
The sharp answer
Putting him in a difficulty
Inquiring about a matter known to be a cause of conflict

The first sample interview (p. 19) begins with the boss reducing the level of anxiety. In the second (p. 22) he is increasing it.

10 RESTATEMENT

A good way to encourage the interviewee to continue explaining a point is to restate it, showing interest, and showing that you understand and sympathize in outline, but would like more detail. For example:

Statement: 'She's not interested in helping me. In fact I think she's got something against me.'

Restatement: 'You think she's got a grudge against you?'

Statement: 'Well, she's very unfriendly, and has been ever since last year.'

Restatement: 'Ever since last year, she's had a grudge?'

Statement: 'Yes, well, I think so. You remember — the time we had to change the figures . . .' (See p. 20)

The boss reflects or echoes what the subordinate has said.

A few points to note:

1 Do not restate so obviously or frequently as to disturb the flow of the interview. The last thing you want is for the subordinate to imagine he has walked into an echo-chamber.

2 Do not be a parrot: use your own words.

3 Do not 'read between the lines', or guess at something left unsaid.

4 Give him plenty of time to reply. He may be groping for words, and is best left to do this himself. If need be, restate the restatement. Do not let his silence lead you to abandon that line of enquiry and start another.

5 If you are repeating facts, do not restate every detail, but sum up the main point or points.

6 If you are restating attitudes or feelings, and he has mentioned several or expressed himself in several ways, restate the last one. Begin the restatement with some such phrase as 'You feel that . . .', or 'It seems to you that . . .'

7 It is nearly always better not to indicate whether you agree or disagree with his statement, or whether or not you believe that his attitude is reasonable. His wish to reach agreement will give him the incentive to produce more explanatory detail.

11   *REDEFINING*

Early in every interview the boss should define the problem
with which the interview is to deal. But during the course of
the interview, the nature of the problem may turn out to be
different from the original definition. The boss should then
redefine it.

One problem may turn out to be several. One aspect of a
problem may be simple to solve, another may need to be
deferred, another may be insoluble.

A subordinate may bring a grievance which is in reality
emotional as well as factual. He states the facts, and his tone
indicates the emotions. The redefining may reduce or
eliminate the emotional part, and concentrate on the facts. If
there is personal hostility, this will be excluded from the
redefinition. The boss then needs to get this redefinition
accepted, with some such question as 'is that right? Have I
covered the main points of your complaint?' The subordinate
will not normally reply: 'No – the main point is that I hate
your guts!'

Redefining is a special case of restating. It will sometimes
serve as an intermediate summary, where the problem has
taken a long time to analyse. Like the intermediate summary,
it serves as a starting-off point for the next 'paragraph' of the
interview.

12 SAMPLE INTERVIEWS

1 *Grievance*

Dick Rowe   Come in, Sam. Just a second while I clear the
Boss   air. (*Clears a space on his desk*) How are you?
                   (*Slowly looks up, sympathetically*)

Sam Steel   (*Furious*) I've had just about enough of those
Subordinate typists. They spend half the day reading sloppy
                   magazines and tarting themselves up, and when
                   it comes to doing an honest piece of typing they
                   get very rude. How can we do our work if they
                   don't pull their weight? They say they're rushed,
                   but whenever I go in, half of them are not
                   working. That supervisor, Mrs Tattle — I'm sure
                   she's to blame. (*Stops for breath*)

D. R.   Have you spoken to Mrs Tattle?

S. S.   Yes I have, but she just backs up the girls. You
                   must speak to her. She'd have to listen to you.

D. R.   When did you speak to her? (*Takes pencil and
                   paper*)

S. S.   I've just come from there. She said she can't
                   promise to have my report on Spacklenuts ready
                   for 10 days, and you know the Export
                   Committee want to read it today week.

D. R.   Did you explain that?

S. S.   Yes, but she says she can't help that. She's not
                   interested in helping me. In fact I think she's got
                   something against me.

19

A/658.31

D. R.   You think she's got a grudge against you?

S. S.   Well, she's very unfriendly, and has been ever since last year.

D. R.   Ever since last year, she's had a grudge?

S. S.   (*Slows down, looks away from Dick Rowe, shifts his feet, mumbles*) Yes, well, I think so. You remember— the time we had to change the figures in the Product Analysis report — she made it pretty clear she blamed me for that.

D. R.   I see. (*Leans closer*) And you think she's still taking it out on you for that.

S. S.   Yes, I think so.

D. R.   Is there any other reason for her unkindness?

S. S.   (*Grunt of contempt*) I don't know. No justifiable reason.

D. R.   She hasn't any *justifiable* reason.

S. S.   Well, no, it's her petty regulations, with this form that she wants filled up with every report, saying who its from, and how many copies on pink paper and all that guff — she's got no right to ask for that, but I do it to oblige her, and when I get the numbers in the wrong column she loves to take it out on me.

D. R.   How many reports have you sent her in the last month?

S. S.   About three, I suppose, some of them . . .

D. R.   (*Interrupting*) About three. Right. Have you filled up her form each time?

S. S.   Well, no. I filled it up once but the other times –

D. R.   Once you filled it up, twice you didn't. Was there any reason for that?

S. S.   It didn't seem necessary. Can she insist on that being completed? I tell them what I want.

D. R.   Yes, but if you were in her shoes, wouldn't you be glad to have typing instructions in writing?

S. S.   No – well, it oughtn't to be necessary.

D. R.   Do you know anyone else who doesn't fill up the forms?

S. S.   No one likes filling them up.

D. R.   (*Repeating the question*) Do you know anyone else who doesn't fill them up?

S. S.   No, I don't.

D. R.   Are the typists as rude to everyone as they are to you?

S. S.   I don't know. (*Pause*) No, possibly not.

D. R.   Well, if you will try to fill up Mrs Tattle's form, I expect they will be polite. Come and see me next week — are you free on Thursday at 10.30?

S. S.   Yes, I think so.

D. R.   — And we'll see if the work is flowing a bit more smoothly.

2   *Reprimand including preparation*

D. R.   (*Alone — thinking aloud*) What am I to do about Sam Steel? I've got to get through to him somehow — to get him to fill up the typists' instructions and submit his reports to the typing pool in good time. Let's see — he's done how many reports? Where are they? This one on Marginal Output, this on the Effect of Tariffs — they were both very delayed; and this last one on the Cost/Productivity Ratio wasn't ready in time to be reviewed by the Export Committee. Yes — I've got the relevant dates; now what will he think? Blame the typists, very likely. Well, they can be difficult and overworked, but he must allow for that. Does he plan his work properly? Not very likely. He must be made to accept responsibility. I spoke to him on — when? (*Looks in diary*) about these delays — three weeks ago. So far, then, I've got (*Ticks off on his fingers*)

1 Previous record — poor
2 Discussion 3 weeks ago
3 No sign of improvement

What sanctions have I got? I can't sack him. I can't demote him. I probably can't frighten him very much. So the negative sanctions are not helpful. What positive sanctions or rewards — team spirit? What does he want to do? Perhaps there is some underlying problem. I'll have to see. Is there any action I could take — closer supervision perhaps? Yes — I might get him to report his progress twice a week, and keep him up to the mark that way. Now — let's set aside half an hour for this. Should be over in that time. I think tomorrow would be a good day — I can ask him what progress he's made on the Barium Draft.

Next day

D. R.   Come in.

S. S.   (*Comes in*) Hello Dick. What was it? (*Sits in chair*)

D. R.   Look — I've got something serious to talk about.

S. S.   Uh-huh.

D. R.   I've had enough of your casual approach. (*Steel tenses up*) I thought when I spoke about 3 weeks ago on the subject of late reports, I would have no more trouble.

S. S.   Late reports? (*He is playing for time*)

D. R.   Yes, do you remember?

S. S.   Do you mean your complaining that the reports weren't ready in time, and that it was my fault?

D. R.   Yes, you do remember, then.

23

S. S.   But I told you. These typists, they sit on their chairs and knit, and every time I ring up and enquire how my draft is going they say they're very busy and haven't time to discuss it. I explained this to you.

D. R.   Yes, but did I accept your explanation?

S. S.   Well, I can't remember.

D. R.   Try. Do you remember anything I said?

S. S.   Well, you said you expected better things.

D. R.   Did I say that it would be all right if the typists continued to delay reports?

S. S.   No, of course not, but it's not my fault.

D. R.   Whose responsibility is it to get the draft ready on time?

S. S.   If the organization doesn't provide enough typists . . .

D. R.   Is it the organization's responsibility?

S. S.   Up to a point, yes.

D. R.   Could you make out a case for more typists?

S. S.   No, I haven't enough information.

D. R.   Well, it's your responsibility, and mine, to get the reports ready on time, or else explain properly why they're delayed. Agreed?

S. S. Yes.

D. R. For your next report I want a plan of how long it will take you, and how long you are allowing to type. I will discuss this with Mrs Tattle, the Senior Typist. And I need a progress report twice a week on whether we are up to schedule or behind schedule starting next Thursday at 10.30 am.

Chapter Two The Selection Interview

1   *AIMS OF THE SELECTION INTERVIEW*

1 To help in the process of choosing people for jobs by

a informing applicants about the jobs
b predicting which applicants will be (i) able and (ii) willing
to do the jobs
c influencing suitable candidates to accept.

2 To show all the applicants, including the failures, that the
Company is a good one, and has tried to be fair. To create a
good 'image', or goodwill.

2   *DRAWBACKS OF THE INTERVIEW*

In addition to the difficulties of conducting any interview,
there are special difficulties with the selection interview:

1 Both sides know that much is at stake. The selection
process is at least as important as the difficulty and cost of
replacing a wrong selection. It is a tense interview.

2 The interview forces employer and applicant into acting.
The employer presents an impression of himself and the job.
The applicant presents an impression of himself and his
ability and enthusiasm. Both may feel they have a vested
interest in suppressing part of the truth and exaggerating
other parts. The winning applicant may be merely the one
who is good at being interviewed.

3 The selection interview is unreliable, in that different
interviewers assess the same candidate differently. The
selection interview is a subjective way of reaching what ought

to be an objective conclusion.

4 The task of predicting how applicants will perform seems difficult. Previous predictions may be known to have been mistaken. The longer-term the prediction, the less valid it is likely to be, and often a selection interviewer has to make a prediction covering the rest of the working life of the applicant.

5 The 'halo effect' is particularly dangerous. The interviewer is disposed to emphasise and exaggerate all a man's qualities because he is struck by one quality. Conversely, an applicant who makes a poor impression at the beginning of the interview casts a shadow over all his later answers.

3   WHAT CAN BE DONE OUTSIDE THE INTERVIEW

The aims of the selection interview (see 1 above) include helping in the process of choosing people for jobs. The process will include much besides the actual interview:

1 Long term organization planning. Every manager should have, locked up if necessary, a projected organization chart for five years ahead, showing what staff he will need then. No doubt, like real organization charts, it will need continuous amendment, and will be always slightly out of date. Every selection should be compatible with the long-term plan. Is it necessary to recruit anyone at all?

2 Advertizing. Consideration of the merits of internal promotion against outside recruitment.

3 The basic answers to the questions

1 What is the job?

2 What kind of a person am I looking for?
3 How will I recognize him when I see him?

These points will be dealt with later in sections 4, 6 and
8 – *Job Description, Man Description,* and *Interview structure.*

4 The statement of aims above defined the ideal applicant as
one who is able and willing. Whether an applicant is *willing* is
probably assessed better inside the interview than outside.
Whether he is *able* can often be assessed objectively, before
the interview. For instance, there are tests of

a intelligence (verbal, numerical, etc)
b health (medical examination)
c imagination (artistic, problem-solving, etc)
d skill (manual dexterity, shorthand, etc)

Film actors submit to screen tests and army officers to tests
of initiative. Probably tests exist for the abilities that any
interviewer will be able to define. The snag is that they take
time to arrange and professional skill to interpret. It would
be as dangerous for an amateur to run and interpret an
intelligence test, as for an amateur to conduct a medical
examination.

5 There are other sources of information besides the
interview:

1 qualifications (academic qualifications are a good substitute
for intelligence tests)
2 details of experience, supported by references
3 the letter of application

4   *JOB DESCRIPTION*

1 Title and context

Job title. Purpose. Grade. Location. Status.
Number of employees in this job. Recognized Trade Union.
Place in organization. To whom responsible. For whom
responsible. Closely related jobs.
Date of Job Description, and date to be revised

2 Pay and terms of contract

Pay: Basic, range, guaranteed minimum, expected
increments, piece rates, incentives, commission, productivity
bonus, average earnings, overtime, superannuation, method
of payment, method of reviewing payment. Sick pay

Expenses: Car, tools, clothes, travelling, accommodation,
removal expenses, subsistence

Fringe benefits: Pensions, luncheon vouchers, discount goods

Deductions: Union, social, welfare, savings schemes

Terms of employment: Hours of work, holidays, period of
probation, period of notice, procedure for dismissal,
procedure for redundancy

3 Duties

Sequence of operations. Standards of quality and output.
Methods. Effort and skill needed. Average proficiency time.
Responsibility for people, interviewing, training, supervising,
dismissing. Keep staff records. Control timekeeping and
absence. Co-operate with Union representatives.
Committees. Responsibility for safety.
Creative work. Art, invention, problem-solving. Beginning
new projects.
Sales. Receiving, telephoning, writing to customers.
Plan. Set output targets. Estimate the work-content of jobs.

Progress work. Check stores. Chase supplies. Work with
equals and superiors. Prepare budgets, keep accounts,
compile tables and graphs, write letters and reports. Speak in
public or to meetings.
Responsibility for cash. Use of, or responsibility for,
machines, repair or maintenance.
Usual difficulties or causes of failure. Usual reasons for job
satisfaction or job distaste.
Method of measuring work progress; job appraisal or other
way of telling job holder of his success

4 Working environment

Ease of getting to and from work, parking, public or firm's
transport; heat, cold, noise, dampness, on job.
Time, irregular or shift work, being 'on call'.
Special or protective clothes. Posture, physical comfort.
Work speed, variety, monotony, eyestrain, nervous strain,
opportunity to rest and smoke. Social or solitary features of
job. Element of danger. Health hazards

5 Training and prospects

Eligibility for training. Time (full or part time), place
(in-Company or external, on or off the job), and kind of
training.
Opportunities for transfer, training, and re-training. Criteria
for transfer, training, and promotion. Method of promotion

5   COMMENTS ON THE JOB DESCRIPTION

This catalogue is no more than a check list which may help
those preparing for a selection interview. Those who are close
to a job can easily overlook some obvious elements if they do
not check their description against such a list. Those who do

not use a Job Description will hardly be able to assess which
are the aspects to remember when it comes to interviewing.

Many of these points will be irrelevant to any one job. Other
points will need elaboration. Some points will be essential,
others desirable. In senior posts, the Job Description becomes
what the holder makes it, because so much is at his
discretion. The Job Description should clarify the job, but
not fossilize it. Even if technical innovation did not require
managers to revise Job Descriptions regularly, labour
turnover would force them to do so. New men with new
attitudes, or even the same men with developing experience,
change the nature of the work they do.

It is logical to consider the Job Description before the kind
of person we need to fill the job. But the process is two-way:
jobs have to fit human beings, as well as human beings fit
jobs. The growing and more civilized practice is to extend the
control that individuals have over their jobs. This does not
make the Job Description unnecessary, but perhaps large
chunks of it need to be marked 'subject to negotiation'.

Once in existence, the Job Description serves many purposes.
It can help the organization by highlighting (taken with other
Job Descriptions) gaps or areas of conflicting overlap. It can
help with work study, and studies of productivity, career
development, pay structure, training needs, and promotion.

The Job Description is tied to one job, but a man is not
necessarily recruited for only one job. Some firms recruit
qualified staff (graduates, for instance) without knowing
which actual job they will do. Sometimes the employer needs
a man to do two or more jobs in sequence, for instance in
planning to replace someone due to retire soon. In order to
find the right man, it will be necessary to collect two or more
Job Descriptions. There is a danger in finding a man who is,

in vague terms, employable at a certain level and salary, and then finding that none of the jobs actually available at his level fit his paricular characteristics. The moral is that even recruitment to a 'grade' covering a range of jobs, should depend on Job Descriptions. It is not enough to say what qualities the successful applicants should have. It is not enough to say that they must be transferable. These statements need to be related to the content of some or all of the alternative jobs, one of which the man will have to occupy.

6   *MAN DESCRIPTION*

1 Is he able?

a physically

Sex, age, weight, height, build, strength, stamina
Hands, legs, eyesight, hearing, nerves
What physical handicaps would be acceptable?
How important is the first impression, good looks, physical co-ordination, way of standing, way of walking?

What physical activities at school would we expect to be relevant? What interests and hobbies would he have? What physical aspects of his previous employment and experience would be relevant?

Is manual dexterity or mechanical dexterity important enough to be worth testing outside the interview?

Do we need a medical examination? If so, what are the specific jobs for which the doctor needs to pass him as medically fit?

b mentally

Intelligence, knowledge, experience, skill, judgment
Original, creative faculties
Critical, judicial faculties

What academic qualifications do we expect? What interests
and hobbies? What subjects and activities at school would he
have been likely to do well?

Is intelligence an important enough factor to justify tests
conducted by an appropriate specialist? Or would the
academic record be a good enough guide to intelligence?
What is the minimum acceptable level of intelligence? Is there
a maximum?

What other skills would be better assessed by tests outside
the interview? Numerical ability, oral ability, verbal skill;
tests of creative imagination, or problem-solving ability; tests
of concise writing

What professional training and qualifications would be
relevant? Should he be able to learn fast?

Should he have previous experience of similar work? What
are the key areas, where previous experience is vital? What
should he have learnt from this experience? What skills
should he have developed?

What organising ability does he need? Should he be able to
organise his own work, or other people's work?

What skills in dealing with people are needed? Carrying out
orders, briefing subordinates, speaking in public, speaking in
committee, interviewing, putting a case to a group?

How far must he conform to the attitudes and behaviour of
the existing team or organization? How much divergence
from the customs and behaviour of the existing team would
interfere with efficiency? How much divergence would be
acceptable? How much would be a useful corrective to a
stereotyped group with a narrow outlook?

Should he have any skills, knowledge, or experience in
reserve, over and above what the job may require?

2 Is he willing?

a ambition

Do we want a man content to stay, or ambitious to move?
What ambitions of the individual would fit career prospects
which the employer could offer?

What motives and 'drives' would be most appropriate?
Money, security and stability; change and variety; popularity;
serving the community; travelling; job interest; developing his
abilities; independence

Would the job be more likely to suit a man or a woman? A
married or a single person? Someone with commitments
(children, a mortgage) or someone without?

What should be his scale of values? Should he be cautious or
courageous, rigid or flexible, a rebel or a conformist? How
much will he have to be trusted? How important is it that he
be truthful; loyal to friends, to equals, to subordinates, to
superiors; reliable; tactful?

What sort of subjects, hobbies, and interests might he have
enjoyed? For instance:

artistic, creative, experimental, original
social, organizational, in teams, in public life
do-it-yourself
collecting and classifying
commercial
educational
mental games, like cards or crosswords

b action

How hard will he have to push himself? How much energy
does the job require? Could someone have too much energy
to do the job satisfactorily?

How much effort should he have put into work at school?
Should his achievement be greater than could be expected
from someone of his intelligence? Should he enjoy working
hard to overcome obstacles? Should we expect to find
evidence of this in his interests or his career?

Should he have worked beyond the duty laid down? Should
he have developed the job? If he has failed to achieve some
ambition, for some reason outside his control, should he be
resigned, or bitterly disappointed?

7   COMMENTS ON THE MAN DESCRIPTION

The Man Description is based on one or more Job
Descriptions. I assume that the interviewer knows the job for
which he is interviewing; it would hardly be possible to
construct a useful Man Description from a Job Description
alone.

The Man Description goes on to form the basis of the
interview, but of more than the interview: of the tests, of the

request for references, of other checks on the qualifications and experience of applicants.

The interviewer needs to predict how far applicants are able, and how far they are willing, to do the required job. It is convenient to divide the Man Description that way, notwithstanding the fact that the same piece of evidence will often prove relevant both to ability and to willingness.

One reason for the division is that there are valuable alternatives to the interview in assessing ability but hardly any alternatives in assessing willingness. In theory there are references. These depend on the attitude of the referees. No doubt an honest referee, with a good memory and the time to write a full reference and the courage to be candid, would give a useful reference. The interviewer would have to know him to be such. In certain professions, or inside one organization, we may get near to these ideal conditions. In practice, an open reference is valueless; a confidential reference is limited by a referee's desire to help the applicant to reform or improve; a 'present boss' reference is affected by the natural wish to hang on to a good man, and help an indifferent one to make a move; a 'past boss' reference is limited by how much the referee remembers, and how much the applicant has changed.

It is likely, therefore, that the greater part of the interview, and the more difficult part, will be concerned with the applicant's willingness. How much does he want to do the job successfully? How much energy will be bring to the task? This part of the Man Description is the most vital for the interviewer.

Do not think of a person as merely a collection of characteristics. One person is a unity which no other person ever fully grasps or can understand. Luckily we do not need fully to understand people in order to employ them effectively.

'I can tell what a man's like as soon as I set eyes on him' is so arrogant and unscientific a statement that few openly make it. Yet we are all prone to put more value on immediate physical characteristics than they are worth. Red hair, blue eyes, brown skin provoke instant emotions, but they are irrelevant unless we are casting a play or running a strip club. Racial discrimination is illegal, but almost all forms of physical discrimination are anti-social. Disabled people are not unemployable, but their successful employment depends on finding them a suitable place. Be careful how you use the argument that 'they would not be acceptable to other employees, or customers' as a reason for not employing applicants of an unpopular race or disability. This is the argument all prejudiced people use, to indulge their prejudice while hiding behind the (often non-existent) prejudices of others. Give some thought to the effect of your decisions on the way society develops, and the reputation of 'management'.

Nearly all the ideal requirements are within a range from minimum to maximum. Avoid simply getting 'the best man we can'; he may be too good for the job. There are limits on the amount of intelligence, knowledge, skill, ambition, and energy that will fit a given job. Whales die in shallow water.

8 INTERVIEW STRUCTURE

1 *Beginning.* Normally, the applicant is nervous, and must be put at ease, and be reassured of sympathetic treatment, or he will not talk freely and fully. The ways of reducing anxiety are described on p. 15, and are useful here. However, there are some other easy ways of reducing anxiety in a selection

interview. Conventionally, the interviewer offers a cigarette; a chocolate, a cup of tea or coffee, or a glass of sherry would be as good.

The interviewer should show a bit of his own personality early on, perhaps by referring to some item of news, or a book on his desk, or something he has done earlier in the day. This is to show that he is human and to reduce tension; clearly it must be friendly, and gentle, or it may have the opposite effect. It would do no good to slap the applicant on the back.

Then the subject may pass to neutral ground about the interview; the applicant's journey, his home, his expenses. There is this to be said for asking him to submit expenses before the interview: they are more likely to be reasonable claims than after the interview, when he may feel that the job is definitely his, or that he has absolutely no chance.

Then should come a few easy limiting questions. These are questions which he will have no difficulty or embarrassment in answering; something like 'How many brothers and sisters have you got?' The more a nervous applicant can hear himself answering confidently, the more his courage will grow.

Sometimes the applicant is not nervous. He may not be interested in the job; in which case the sooner that fact is agreed the less time is wasted. But he may be a first-class man, able to take his pick of jobs; the interviewer will be able to curtail these moves to put him at ease, and give more time to the applicant's questions.

It seems unlikely that the interviewer would ever have deliberately to raise the level of anxiety, at a selection interview.

2 *Probes*. Use the interview papers (the Man Specification, the application form, and references) to identify areas which would repay scrutiny. Do not ignore difficult or embarrassing areas, but leave them until the second half of the interview.

Most areas for probing can be dealt with according to a simple pattern. Start with a statement, taken either from the application form, or from a previous statement of his. Follow this straight away with a limiting question. Listen to his answer. Then put an open question. By now his mind should have focussed on the area you are looking at, and he should give a long answer. When he has finished, sum up his answer, emphasizing any point that you want to pursue. You can then repeat the pattern with another statement.

It might go as follows:

'You have put down stamp collecting as one of your interests. How many years have you been collecting stamps?'

'I started about 20 years ago.'

'What is the appeal of stamps? Why do you collect them?'

Then he might give a long answer which you could sum up as:

'So what started as a simple hobby has become a useful source of income.'

All the time the interviewer must keep control of the interview, be friendly, and keep the level of anxiety down. If the applicant is longwinded, he must be prepared to interrupt one answer with another question. He should keep an eye on the time. He should not let the applicant think he is being cross-examined; a check on the consistency of the applicant's answers should be either apologetic or subtle.

It will often be necessary to take notes during the interview.
Take as few as possible, as it disturbs the flow, takes up time,
and raises the tension. Refer to the fact that you are taking
notes, and apologise for it if you like. Do not take a note
immediately after he has made a mistake or been unable to
answer a question; ask another easy question, and then make
a note. Allow time to take notes immediately after the
interview, which you will use when choosing the successful
applicant.

3 *The job*. The applicant may reasonably expect to find out
more about the vacancy during the interview. Much can be
done before the interview, in the advertisement, or in
duplicated particulars sent to all applicants. You could use
either of these as the framework for talking about the jobs.
You could give him a copy of the Job Description, but this
may contain too much information for him to take in, or
some information that you do not want to reveal to all the
applicants.

There are two main purposes in this part of the selection
interview. The first is to provoke questions for the next part
of the interview. The second is to prevent the successful
applicant saying, six months after accepting the job, 'They
never told me about this side of the work.'

It is not difficult to provoke questions. It may be enough to
describe what is obviously only half of one aspect, and say
that if he is interested you will answer any questions.
The problem of preventing the successful applicant from
feeling that he has not been treated fairly, that some vital
part of his work, or some intractable problem, has been kept
from him, is much more difficult. Plainly there is not enough
time to discuss every aspect of the job in detail. The

interviewer has to select what is important, and his judgment may differ from the applicant's on what is important.

Moreover, most of us do change our tune according to how much we want the applicant. If we have decided against him, we emphasize the unpleasant aspects of the job, to persuade him to withdraw, or to make it easier for him to bear a failure. There is not necessarily anything wrong in that. But the opposite, of telling the applicant we favour all the glamorous parts of the job, even exaggerating them, and playing down the unpleasant or problem parts, is unfair and unsafe. If he is thus tricked into accepting the post, and slowly discovers the truth, he will lose the trust and respect for his employer which is the basis of an effective working relationship.

For instance, it is dangerous to let a gifted man think he is all set for rapid promotion, as a way of inducing him to accept a job below his present ability. All parties to any discussion tend to remember the bits of the discussion that suit them, or excite them. They forget the parts that they want to forget. A selection interviewer may think he has covered himself by being vague, or by a few 'ifs' and 'buts'. The applicant will probably imagine that he is really being recruited for higher posts, not for the advertised one.

4 *Invite questions.* This can be the most revealing part of the interview. A man who is about to commit himself to a new job is making a more important move than an organization that is about to commit itself to a new employee. He is surely entitled to discover at least as much about his job as his employer is entitled to find out about him. He should get a chance during the office interview, and (which may be more fruitful) a chance during a walk round the workplace.

The applicant's questions are revealing too: they tell the

interviewer about the applicant's worries and hopes, experience and interests, his ignorance, or his insight into the job.

5 *Ending*. An efficient interviewer will end his interview when he as no more questions to ask and none to answer, or when his time is up, whichever is earlier. The purpose that he has to remember is to give the applicants a feeling of having had a fair hearing from a good employer. He should thank them. He should make it clear what happens next, be it another interview, or the payment of expenses, or a letter giving the result of the interview. This should be automatic, and may sound perfunctory, like the opening sentences of the interview. But the end of the interview, like the beginning and the middle, must combine good manners with a feeling of direction and purpose.

9   *QUESTIONS FOR SELECTION INTERVIEWING*

Preliminary chit-chat

1   Have a cigarette?
2   Did you have a good journey?
3   What were your travelling expenses?
4   How do you like living in . . .?

Transition

5   What do you know about our Company? (Tell him a bit more)

Previous record

6   Did you like school?
7   What was your favourite subject? Why?

8 Did you decide to become a . . . while you were at school?
9 Which of your jobs have you enjoyed most?
10 What was the best part of that job?
11 Did you get any valuable experience working with . . .?
12 Are you glad you changed from . . . to . . .?

Personality

13 What are your main interests, apart from work?
14 What books have you read lately?
15 Where would you choose to live, ignoring the possibility
   of employment?
16 Who is your favourite character in history?
17 Do you think the mini-skirt is here to stay?
18 What ambitions have you in work or social life? Do you
   see yourself in . . . years' time in any particular job?

The vacancy

19 Had you any particular reason for applying for this job?
20 Do you mind . . .? (Mention some of the drawbacks. Then
   describe the job)
21 Is that fairly clear? Would you like to ask me any
   questions?

Family

22 Have you thought about moving house if you are
   appointed?
23 Will your wife and children be affected by the change?
24 Can we help you with the move (loans, suggestions, etc.)?

Conclusion

25 Thank you for the trouble you have taken
26 We will be writing to you within . . . days

10   *AFTER THE INTERVIEW*

1 Take notes on each applicant after each interview.

2 After all the interviews for one vacancy, ask yourself whether you have a number of applicants who would do the job well; or none who would do the job well; or one or two who would do it well, and the rest clearly less suitable.

3 If you have several who would be good, go through the Job Description, and imagine each good applicant performing the various duties. You are looking for the man who has the best 'extra' contribution to make.

4 If you have none who would do the job well, you have to decide whether to appoint no one, or appoint the applicant who is least unsatisfactory. Go through the Job Description and imagine each applicant performing the various duties. Eliminate the ones who are so unsuitable that you would prefer not to appoint them. If there are any left, look for the one whose limitations would be easiest to tolerate, or whose limitations could be most easily overcome by guidance, training, or re-defining the scope of the job.

5 If one or two stand out, the selection process is relatively easy.

6 Remember the 'Long term organization plan' (see p. 27).

7 Keep some notes on the successful applicant for about six months. Then compare your verdict on him based on the interview, with your verdict based on six months' work. This is a check on all parts of the selection process, but especially the interview.

8 Write to the applicants, and do whatever else you agreed at

the interview to do.

9 Arrange for the successful applicant to receive his Contract of Employment.

10 Arrange an induction interview for his first working day.

11   *THE PANEL INTERVIEW*

In many organizations, particularly large organizations, the selection interview is conducted not by one person but by a panel of three or four (though I have heard of much larger panels). One of the panel is chairman. Usually one is concerned with the job directly, whose task is to ask the technical questions. One is concerned with Personnel policy: pay, holidays, training and so forth.

The advantages of a panel interview are:

1 A panel emphasises the importance and seriousness of the occasion. This should mean that the interviewers put more thought and effort into the interview.

2 The members of the panel can correct each other; if one mis-hears or misunderstands what the applicant says, the others can put him right.

3 The important responsibility for interviewing and selecting is shared. If the selection is successful, all can take credit. If it proves unsuccessful, no one person can be singled out as blameworthy. It is worth noticing that organizations which are accustomed to collective responsibility, and to taking important decisions in committee (the Civil Service, local government, academic bodies) favour the panel; industry, which is used to executives taking individual responsibility,

usually has one-to-one interviews.

4 The panel may obtain some advantage from the division of labour. If each member of the panel specializes in one aspect, he may be able to ask better questions, and give better answers when the applicant asks, than any one person who had to deal with the whole field.

5 The chairman could make it his duty to ensure that members of the panel had done their homework on the applications before the interview.

12   DISADVANTAGES OF THE PANEL INTERVIEW

1 Cost. If the panel has four members, one hour of interviewing costs four (probably expensive) man-hours of interviewers' time.

2 The panel arrangement is inflexible in various ways. The time of the interview has to suit more people. If the time is fixed, the most suitable people may not be available. It may be impossible, or difficult, to get the same panel to meet again the next day; so panels are much more likely than individuals to select a candidate on the same day as the interview, which restricts the opportunity to think it over. If one member of the panel, or one applicant, is late or does not come, the time of more people is wasted. If the short-listed applicants are all to be interviewed in sequence by the same panel, they will have to wait together nervously in some waiting-room until they are called. And if the panel intend to offer the job the same day, they will have to wait nervously together after the interview as well.

3 It is more difficult to put the applicant at ease when he is so obviously out-numbered. They can all keep their eyes on

him at once; he can only watch one of them at a time. If the panel all sit on one side of a table, and the applicant sits on the other side, the proceedings resemble an Inquisition.

4 The art of chairmanship is as difficult as the art of interviewing. For instance, if the chairman forgets the time, he may not allocate it fairly among the panel members, or may hog the questions himself. On the other hand, if he keeps strictly to an agreed programme, other members may find that they cannot pursue an interesting point because the chairman has intervened to bring in someone else.

5 Each member of the panel thinks about the other members when he is asking questions, and not just about the job or the applicant. They are tense, because they do not want to say anything that the rest of the panel might think foolish. They may be inclined to show off by using sophisticated terms or talking about their own work. Some panels have to spend the first ten minutes putting themselves at ease, before they put the applicant at ease. The more people there are the longer it takes to find a 'wavelength' in common.

13   *INTERVIEWS IN SERIES*

It may be possible to give the candidate a series of one-to-one interviews, one after the other. It will take more of his time, but probably not significantly more in proportion to the total time he has given up to attend. It is likely to be more fruitful in proportion to the interviewers' time. In fact it has most of the advantages of the panel interview, while avoiding most of the disadvantages.

Chapter Three The Interview at Work

1   *THE INDUCTION INTERVIEW*

After the embarrassment of selection, when the applicant was
on his best behaviour, comes the offer and acceptance of a
job. From then on, the applicant can (relatively anyway)
relax. He has made it. The first important interview he will
have in this state will probably be with his new boss. I call
this the induction interview.

Large firms have induction courses. These are an excellent
way of telling numbers of recruits the broad facts about their
new place of work. It is an induction into the firm; as well as
this, the recruit needs an interview as an induction into his
particular job.

This interview is the foundation-stone of a sound relation
between a subordinate and his boss. It is used by each to find
the other's wavelength. It is true that both may have met and
talked during the selection process; but exchanges then need
to be extended and confirmed now that their new
relationship has begun.

The induction interview may overlap with the instruction or
counselling interview. The manager will find it pays to take
the interview slowly and seriously; his new recruit will be
able to make a useful contribution sooner.

But he should try to remember what the first day in a new
job was like for him. The interviewer finds it easy to go on
talking, but the new man does not take in much. Ideally, the
manager should fill in some of the background, and leave
most of the time for the new man to ask questions.

48

Aims

1 To help an employee to fit in with a new working group
2 To get to know him
3 To sort out any problems on his mind
4 To give him confidence in his leader
5 To help him do the job

Preparation

1 Plan the whole of the first day, if possible, before planning the interview
2 Investigate the interviewee; consult previous interviewers and correspondence
3 Plan the locations and timing; so long in an office, so long walking round the site
4 See that those to whom he should be introduced are available
5 Ensure privacy for the office part of the interview

Structure

1 Congratulate and welcome
2 Ask if he has any problems
3 Explain the day's programme and purpose
4 The job (Is there a written Job Description?)
5 The people
6 The amenities
7 The local customs
8 Sum up
9 Any questions?

Check results

1 Does the employee seem contented?
2 Is he working efficiently?

3 Does he fit in?
4 Did the interview suggest that he needed 'watching' or
  guidance on any special point? Did he really need it? Has
  he received it?
5 Give him a further chance to ask questions at a follow-up
  interview

2   THE GRIEVANCE INTERVIEW

Men in authority do not usually welcome grievances. We all
have defensive emotional reactions which are basic and
strong, and which lead us instinctively to deny a criticism
instead of turning it to our own advantage. In some
emergencies, a critic of authority does more harm than good,
but normally a grievance is valuable feedback that something
has gone wrong. We should overcome our instincts, and thank
the man who brings a grievance. If it is not a justified one,
the manager can take the chance to put the grapevine
straight.

The manifest or declared grievance may not be the extant or
real grievance. The manager would be wise not to dismiss
someone's grievance simply because it is plainly false. He
should try to establish the real grievance. There is a tradition
that complaints about canteen food signify poor morale or
worsening industrial relations. Strikes over wage differentials
are less because of the actual money, which is often little
enough, than because of what the differentials symbolize:
status.

A man with a private worry which he is unsure whether to
discuss with his manager, may use an artificial grievance as a
way of securing the manager's attention. The manager should
use questioning, restating, and redefining techniques
carefully, in a friendly and encouraging way, to turn a bogus

grievance interview into a genuine counselling interview.
The initiative in this interview rests with the person with a
grievance. The manager should therefore cultivate the habit
of doing the 'preparation' in the first minutes of a
spontaneous grievance interview.

Remember that angry men can be calmed more easily by
action, or planned action than by apologies. And counter-
criticism is, emotionally at least, counter-productive.

Aims

1 To end the grievance, and so improve morale
2 If the grievance is justified, to remove the cause and so
   improve efficiency

Preparation

1 Take time to investigate, if possible
2 Clarify your own rights and powers, and what is the
   company policy
3 Ensure privacy

Structure

1 Welcome the grievance
2 Listen to the grievance
3 Restate it in your own words
4 Get assent to your restatement
5 Give your own interpretation of the facts
6 Say what you have done so far
7 Say what you intend to do, but do not limit your freedom
   to manoeuvre if something unexpected occurs
8 Give reasons for your interpretation and action
9 End on a note of appreciation and sympathy

Check results

1 Check morale
2 Check that the grievance has ended, and no substitute grievance has arisen
3 Check relations and attitude
4 Check performance and efficiency

3   *THE INSTRUCTION INTERVIEW*

Using the interview to instruct is common enough, particularly among staff whose work normally includes interviews for other purposes. It is perhaps not normally considered as one of the kinds of interview, because instruction is traditionally either 'sitting next to Nellie' or else something that goes on in a classroom.

Nevertheless the interview is a concentrated and effective kind of instruction. It corresponds to private tuition. It is ideal for individuals who do not want their ignorance exposed to a class. It is necessary when only one person needs the lesson. It may be the only way to put across something that depends on individual reactions: how to handle a difficult subordinate, or how to put a case to a committee or a customer.

The instruction interview can arise from the progress interview. It is closely related to the correction interview.

Aims

1 To get a job done well and willingly
2 To draw out the abilities of the individual

Preparation

1 Establish the extent of the job
2 Consider how the job fits into the work of the whole
  organization
3 Consider how the job fits into the career and development
  of the individual
4 Prepare examples for demonstration or other visual aids
5 Consider the points that most need emphasis
6 Plan the instruction; make notes
7 Establish when he will be carrying out the instruction
8 Decide how closely his performance should be supervised

Structure

1 State purpose of the interview
2 State how the job fits into the work of the whole
  organisation
3 Define the job; demonstrate if possible
4 Invite questions and answer them
5 Recapitulate the difficult or important points
6 Express confidence in his ability to perform it

Check results

1 Check performance of job
2 If done well, congratulate; if not, consider correction or
  reprimand

4   THE CORRECTION INTERVIEW

I have distinguished between the correction and the reprimand, as these two types of interview need different treatment. To receive a reprimand, an individual must be clearly blameworthy; if he has done wrong but it is not his fault, because (for instance) he has been badly trained, the interview should be a correction.

A person who makes a mistake has a tendency to confuse the correction and the reprimand. First, he is annoyed at the error, and its discovery, even (perhaps especially) if it is not his fault. It can be difficult to put someone right without appearing to criticize. If an innocent and sensitive person detects the least sign of unjustified criticism, he may 'counter-attack' sharply, or alternatively nurse a grudge, according to temperament. He has interpreted a correction as a reprimand. On the other hand, someone receiving a reprimand has a vested interest in interpreting it as a correction. He may have done something incorrectly, but if it was someone else's fault, his pride is not wounded.

The interviewer must sort out both sorts of confusion.

Aims

1 To improve performance
2 To prevent repetition
3 To protect others from carelessness or danger

Preparation

1 Remember that, unlike a reprimand, the individual is not to be blamed
2 Take time to investigate, if possible, and see where the blame lies. If it is partly your own fault, admit it briefly

3 Take action outside the interview to prevent repetition of the mistake
4 Correct rather than reprimand for
  a trivial errors
  b first offences without grave consequences
  c individuals in a new job or procedure; old habits may be asserting themselves, or he may have been badly instructed, or not have had enough experience
5 Plan the correction as a piece of training

Structure

1 Point out the error
2 State that no blame is attached. Take the blame yourself if you can do so sincerely; be brief
3 Explain the effects of the error
4 Demonstrate the correct method, in a way suitable to the individual
5 Ask questions
6 Make sure correction is understood and accepted
7 Encourage self-correction

Check results

1 See mistake is not made again
2 If it is, consider reprimanding. If it is not, congratulate
3 Give an opportunity to ask questions which occurred to him after the interview was over

5 THE REPRIMAND INTERVIEW

The aims of the reprimand are the same as the aims of the correction. The aim is not to punish (though that may be a way of achieving the aim), nor is it to pass moral judgement; these are at best means. And the only effective means is for the man to reprimand himself, to convict himself. If he does not plead guilty, the interview becomes a fruitless conflict.

This interview is the manager's most difficult and unpleasant task. It can be a severe strain on the loyalty which a man feels for his colleagues. But it is part of the manager's job. A boss who cannot reprimand is as useless as one who cannot give orders. The first point for the manager to grasp is that it is part of the work; that it will cut across social relationships; that loyalty to the firm must sometimes outweigh loyalty to a friend. The second point is that he must develop the skill required.

The reprimand is charged with emotion. Yet here above all the man in authority must not lose his temper. In a reprimand there is no room for heated argument, only for a cold, realistic statement of disagreeable facts.

Aims

1 To improve performance
2 To prevent repetition
3 To protect others from carelessness or danger

Preparation

1 Be sure of your ground
2 Take time to investigate, including the man's previous record

3 Plan reprimand in relation to the individual
4 Reprimand in private, subject to the next point
5 Consider bringing in your Personnel Department, and the
   man's Trade Union

Structure

1 Get to the point at once
2 Get agreement on the facts. Be exact
3 Get admission of the offence
4 Do not argue
5 Give him a chance to reply fully
6 See he understands the consequences of his behaviour
   a to his colleagues (the reasons behind the rules)
   b to himself (disciplinary sanctions)
   c to his ideal of himself (self-esteem)
7 Show him how to improve and show confidence in his
   ability to do so

Check results

1 See error does not recur
2 Do not show antagonism
3 Check his attitude and relationships
4 Check his work generally

6   THE COUNSELLING INTERVIEW

Sometimes a manager must be a social worker. By a counselling interview, I mean something which goes outside the normal working relationship between a manager and his subordinate. Organizations are made up of human beings, who bring to work not only their hands and their brains, for the service of their employer, but also their private worries.

An employee in the grip of drugs or debt is seldom able to see the way out. He needs help from someone he trusts, who can see the problem dispassionately. Sometimes the manager can solve the problem and lay it on the table, pat. Sometimes he knows who can help. Sometimes it is enough to be a sympathetic audience, while the subordinate thinks out loud, and so solves the problem himself.

In this interview, the manager's authority comes not from the status which the organization bestows on him, but from the trust of the subordinate. If the manager abuses this trust, the working relationship will suffer, just as until the problem is solved, the subordinate's work will suffer.

Difficult cases can waste a lot of the manager's time. He needs the skill to reserve time and energy for his own job, without being unfriendly or brusque to someone less fortunate than himself. Large firms, recognizing the dilemma, have Welfare Officers to deal with such cases. But whether or not there is a Welfare Officer, the manager must learn some of the social worker's skills.

Here are a few guiding principles:

1 Tell no one what the subordinate has told you, unless he has given you permission, or unless there is some higher moral principle involved. Respect his confidence

2 Do not put words in his mouth; let him tell his own story
3 If you must advise, put it in the form of a question: 'Have you thought of going to the Citizen's Advice Bureau?'

Aims

1 To help employees solve their problems concerning work or their private life
2 To improve performance and working relationships by helping solve these problems

Preparation

1 If possible, set aside so much time that the interview does not have to be cut short
2 Ensure privacy
3 Consider the person's background (education, home, work) and what problems he might have
4 Consider what other persons or agencies (medical, social, legal, etc.) might help
5 Consider how his work would be done if he had to have leave of absence

Structure

1 Welcome and put at ease
2 Let him state his problem
3 Redefine the problem, analysing it into different problems where necessary
4 Take each problem separately. Use short questions to get him to expand
5 Listen sympathetically
6 Contribute your knowledge of the persons or agencies to whom he could turn for help
7 Help him to formulate a plan of action

8 Assure him of your help, and that his affairs will be kept
  secret
9 Arrange a follow-up interview   ﹒

Check results

1 Hold the follow-up interview. This time five minutes may
  be enough

7   THE TERMINATION INTERVIEW

When a person resigns his job, he is in a good position to give
constructive feedback about the organization he has worked
for. He can comment without fear of reprisals, and so his
views will be free in a way that is hardly possible while he is
in continuing employment.

A good manager will not neglect this opportunity. Many
firms collect 'Reasons for Leaving' on a form, which every
leaver completes, and the reasons are later fitted into
categories and presented as a table of statistics at the end of
the year. But these reasons are at best superficial. An
interview will get much closer to the truth than a form.

Finding out the background reasons for the resignation is
part of the purpose of a termination interview, so that similar
resignations can be made less likely in future. But it is only
part. Even those who have a very obvious reason (promotion
to a better job than they could obtain by staying put, or a
husband who is moving out of the area) are worth
interviewing. It may be that the firm are recruiting people
too well qualified or too ambitious for the job. Those who
are content in their move will make the more constructive
and less embittered comments.

Where there is some bitterness, it may help if the termination interview is not conducted by the leaver's immediate boss. Some organizations arrange for a Personnel Officer to interview leavers; sometimes a manager other than the immediate boss may do it. Where the firm chooses to make a determined effort to persuade someone to withdraw his resignation, two or three interviews may be needed; and several interviews may be helpful in obtaining information even where there is no hope of keeping the person.

This interview would hardly be appropriate for someone who had been dismissed.

Aims

1 To improve the efficiency of the selection process
2 To remedy any organization problems
3 To reduce staff turnover
4 To persuade the leaver to withdraw his resignation if appropriate
5 To improve the image of the organization in the leaver's mind

Preparation

1 Study the history of the leaver
2 Consider his recent performance and behaviour
3 Speak to his supervisor
4 Consider what you know of his home background

Structure

1 Welcome and put at ease
2 Express regret at resignation
3 State purpose of interview

4 Ask reasons for leaving and general comments
5 Restate his points, and get assent to restatement
6 Correct any errors of fact
7 Make notes of serious points
8 Indicate what you will do towards preventing a recurrence
9 Offer thanks and good wishes

Check results

1 Revise the Job Specification and Man Specification for the leaver's job
2 Act on the points made in the interview
3 Check morale of those in similar jobs

Chapter Four The Progress Interview

1 WHAT IS A PROGRESS INTERVIEW?

Whenever a boss and his subordinate meet, just the two of
them, to discuss how the subordinate is making progress, we
have the kernel of a progress interview.

It is the most complex and difficult kind of interview to
conduct. It calls for all the skills required at the other types
of interview. It is usually made up of different strands,
serving different purposes, combined in one interview. We
discuss here the different strands, but this is not to suggest
that it is possible to combine them all in one interview.
Which strands are separated into different interviews, and
which are combined, will depend on particular circumstances.

If the interview is not to be a pointless embarrassment, the
interviewer must have a clear idea of his purpose, and of the
dangers.

2 AIMS OF THE PROGRESS INTERVIEW

These aims can include one or more of the following:

1 To improve individual performance by knowledge of
   results
2 To reconcile the man's ambitions with the employer's
   objectives
3 To improve communication between boss and subordinate
4 To help an individual to see and overcome his failings
5 To help the manager to take stock of his subordinate's
   work

6 To help the manager to see and overcome *his* failings
7 To help the subordinate to develop his talents
8 To give recognition of good work
9 To prevent the recurrence of old difficulties
10 To help the employer with his manpower planning
11 To identify outstanding men early in their career
12 To assist the employer's salary administration
13 To help with the employer's redundancy or dismissal procedure
14 To plan future work, and set targets or objectives

3 *DRAWBACKS OF THE PROGRESS INTERVIEW*

1 Boss and subordinate are frightened of changing their previous relationship.

2 In particular, boss and subordinate normally have a friendly social relationship, in addition to their working relationship. How do you joke with a man one day and the next day tell him he will not be recommended for promotion? How do you preserve the boss-subordinate relationship, without jeopardising the other happier, and more equal, relationship?

3 If there is some grievance or conflict between the two, smouldering beneath the surface, this interview may cause it to explode, hurting both without resolving the cause.

4 Reserved people, as Englishmen often are, only talk about important things with difficulty and embarrassment.

5 The subordinate may be more quick witted at interviews than the boss. This frightens the boss, and may frustrate the purpose of the interview.

6 Where the boss judges the subordinate, the judgment will be subjective. The 'halo effect' (see p. 27) applies to progress as well as selection.

7 The truth may be merely depressing. For instance, to tell a man that his hopes of advancement have been groundless may cause his morale and performance to suffer rather than improve.

4   *HOW NOT TO DO IT*

In some organizations, the subordinates look forward to their progress interview keenly, but their managers are shy of it.

The subordinate may spend days, or even weeks, anticipating the interview; fearing it perhaps; working out carefully every word he means to say; examining his conduct over the year; framing questions to ask.

The boss also fears the interview, but in his case it is more difficult to say why. He makes little preparation. He conducts the interview at Christmas, when it can be linked to an annual salary review, and to 'tidings of comfort and joy'. With a skilful secretary he hopes to get through ten or more interviews a day, on top of his normal work.

It is tragic that all the subordinate's concentration and energy, and all the potential for discussion, support, recognition and improvement, which could benefit both the individual and his employer, should be wasted.

5   PROGRESS OR APPRAISAL?

The word 'appraisal' is commonly used to describe this
interview, but it seems to me to be open to an important
objection. It puts the emphasis on 'evaluating' the
subordinate, and evaluation is not an important part of the
purpose. It may well not help towards achieving any of the
purposes. If it is interpreted literally, it dehumanizes the
relations between interviewer and interviewee.

The *Shorter Oxford English Dictionary* defines the words as
follows:

Progress. A dozen meanings, including 'advance,
advancement; growth, development; usu. in good sense,
continuous improvement'

Appraisal. 'The act of appraising; the setting of a price'

Appraise. '1. To fix a price for; esp. as an official valuer. 2.
To estimate the amount, or worth of'

Human beings do not want to be priced like a second-hand
car. Managers do not want to be 'official valuers'.

An interview would not be necessary for that purpose at all.
The object of the interview is the growth and development it
encourages, and the name of the interview ought to
emphasize this aspect.

The word 'appraisal' reinforces the myth that a man's work
can be marked like an examination paper, and that the total
mark is all that matters. A 'good' man becomes one with a
high mark, and the human race can be strung out along a
one-dimensional spectrum. The marks relate to a man's

earnings. A manager becomes entitled to 'judge' or 'appraise' his subordinates because he has more marks and is therefore a better man. All men work (the theory says) for more money or promotion, which become synonymous. The person with the highest mark of all becomes Prime Minister.

If this is ridiculous, why do so many 'appraisal' schemes seem to be based on this kind of theory?

Many Companies, and the Civil Service, have some Assessment Form, or Report, about their staff, connected to their promotion policy, their manpower planning and career development. When they decide (as is commonly the case) to impose an appraisal or progress interview on all their managers, it is linked to this Form or Report. For administrative simplicity, managers have to tick boxes beside various qualities, each box representing such comments or evaluations as 'outstanding', 'average', or 'unsatisfactory'. Managers have to be 'official valuers'. And because the forms are used for a wide range of people in a wide range of jobs, the qualities tend to be vague: 'Technical understanding', 'A good influence', or 'Shows initiative'.

These forms may then be used to plan the career development of individuals. At this point another snag arises: if the 'official valuer' knows that his evaluation will be used like this, and affect a career, he changes the attitude to the Form, and indeed changes his values, just as commercial valuers will give a minimum value for probate and a maximum for insurance.

Plainly we need at least two valuations, one for the administrative appraisal and another for the progress interview. If the administrative system, or the interview, concerns itself with the chances of promotion or transfer, we need a further subdivision. The value of a man in his present

67

job does not necessarily relate to his value in another job. An average craftsman might become a first class supervisor. Equally, we do not take our best surgeons, and reward them for their excellent surgery by taking them away from the operating table and inviting them to administer a chain of hospitals. Industry does sometimes make this kind of mistake, and unless the system guards against the tendency, it will be likely to imply that all outstanding performers ought to be promoted.

What right, anyway, has the manager to make this appraisal? Was he in fact promoted because he was a good judge of others, a good appraiser? His valuation will reflect his temperament. Personnel departments which collate these valuations know that they tell you as much about the appraiser as the man appraised. No doubt if all a manager's geese are swans (or vice versa) the system will spot it and make the necessary correction. Less easy to identify is the effect of personal sympathy or antagonism between a manager and one particular subordinate.

And if, in the interview, the manager communicates his evaluation or appraisal to the subordinate, how will it help the subordinate to develop or grow? The subordinate may agree with the appraisal. If the appraisal is critical, this could lead to despair, and if the appraisal is flattering, to complacency. If the subordinate disagrees, he is unlikely to benefit from the appraisal. The possible consequences include open conflict, a silent grudge, and loss of confidence in the appraiser.

There is more sense in the idea that men in jobs are pegs of odd shapes in holes of odd sizes. 'Progress' does not mean putting a peg into a bigger hole; at least, not necessarily. It is much more a case of finding a peg and a hole that nearly fits; of moulding the pegs (or, as they are human, enabling and encouraging them to mould themselves) to fit in the holes they prefer; and adapting the holes to fit the pegs. This is more complicated and difficult than just 'the setting of a price', but it is also more rewarding.

The job of the progress interview is in many ways like the job of the selection interview. We saw there that it made little sense to look for the 'best' man, and it was necessary to find the man most suited to the job. Let us abandon the idea of marking people, or setting a price on them. The interviewer, the boss, is the representative of the employer at the progress interview. He should concern himself with finding a job, within the limits of the employer's power, which suits the subordinate, which uses his capacities to the full, and which extends the amount of his job that he enjoys and does well.

6 BOSS-BASED OR SUBORDINATE-BASED?

Imagine a progress interview which is entirely 'boss-based': the whole contribution and control comes from the boss. He completes a Company Assessment form. He pronounces on the qualities and shortcomings of the subordinate. He summons the subordinate to his office at a time of his choosing. He tells the subordinate as much of his assessment as he judges is good for the subordinate. If he thinks it is necessary or will help, he refers to possible salary increases or promotion, or to transfer or dismissal. He may support his verdict by evidence he has chosen, to indicate how the subordinate's performance compares with the targets and expectations of the boss. He sets targets and objectives for the future.

Now consider a subordinate-based interview. First, if the subordinate does not want an interview, he does not have one. The subordinate completes his own assessment form. He may devise a form to suit himself. He marks his achievements against the targets which he, the subordinate, originally set. Where he has failed to reach those targets, he gives his reasons. He suggests ways of overcoming his shortcomings, and asks for training or other support from his boss or employer. He chooses the time and place of the interview, which may be at his own place of work. At the interview, he communicates all this to his boss. He asks for transfer or promotion, or he may threaten resignation. He sets targets for the future.

Both these caricatures have their justification. The first resembles a law court, the second a confessional. As in a court, the first interview holds the subordinate captive. As the judge represents society, so the boss represents the organization. In the second interview, the initiative rests with the person being judged, as in the confessional. The courts can use external pressure to force a man to conform; the confessional changes a man from within. But these analogies must not be pressed too far. Managers have no prison. The most powerful sanction they have is probably people's self-esteem or vanity. But they have got a large organization whose interests it is their duty to protect, and they should be in a better position to 'judge' what needs doing, and how to do it, than a subordinate. So there may be a time and place for either of these two methods.

Usually the important thing is to get agreement between both parties. Without this progress is hardly possible. Both the boss-based interview and the subordinate-based interview do not adequately allow for this. Where the boss is dealing with young or inexperienced subordinates, the boss-based interview may be nearer the mark. Where both parties are mature and co-operative, the subordinate may draw up the agenda and do most of the talking. Probably the ideal is some half-way house between the two extremes.

7   SHORT-TERM REVIEWS

In some jobs work is easily measured and close control and
feedback is important; in sales or production, for instance.
For this purpose a manager may hold regular meetings with
all his team. These regular meetings are sometimes called
'briefing meetings' or 'briefing groups', which emphasizes that
the boss is informing subordinates of future plans. But this is
also a function of the progress interview, and briefing groups
can include on a group level most of the other facets of
progress interviews. Where the work suggests individual
progress interviews rather than team meetings, the aims and
content of such interviews will resemble the aims and content
of 'briefing groups'.

These short-term progress interviews may be held monthly,
weekly, or even daily. They aim to improve performance by
analysing progress since the last interview. The existence of
the interview is an incentive to the subordinate to do his best.
Where progress is not satisfactory, both boss and subordinate
are responsible for remedying the situation, and may best do
this by discussion.

Among the subjects covered will be:

1 Progress since the last interview
2 Any necessary remedial action
3 Decisions by higher management which affect the work of
  the subordinate
4 Targets to be achieved before the next interview
5 Any questions or suggestions

One approach is to have meetings or interviews of this kind
frequently but not regularly. Instead of having a 'Monday
morning prayer meeting' or a 'First Tuesday in the month'
type of fixture, they only hold a meeting when there is a

specific item to discuss. They may have two interviews in one week, and then none for a month.

Although such irregular interviews may be supposed to save time, they have disadvantages. Most of us, when we get a message that the boss wants to see us, think instinctively 'What have I done wrong now?', try to guess what the accusation will be, and prepare our excuses. If the interview was expected, we would come to it in a less defensive, and more receptive, frame of mind. And subordinates will be able to save up less urgent grievances for the expected meeting, when they will be able to put them with more care, and less emotionally, than if they have to raise them unexpectedly.

If the frequency is correctly established (daily, weekly, or monthly) there will always be some of the subjects suggested above which will be worth discussing. It is up to the boss to see that the time is not wasted discussing something that would not be discussed, and that no one would want to discuss, were it not for the interview.

These short-term progress interviews are not usually imposed on a manager by the organization. They are up to the individual manager and his particular circumstances. In this respect they are rather different from the long-term interview.

8   LONG-TERM REVIEWS

Much that we have said about short-term reviews applies equally to long-term. They should be regular, and expected; they should include in principle what the short-term interviews include. But as they are held at longer intervals, annually or every six months, perhaps, they have a different character. They tend to be more elaborate, they discuss more fundamental things, they focus on the progress of the individual and his career. This all makes them more difficult to handle.

If a boss holds both short-term and long-term interviews, the long-term interview will start from the base of the short-term interviews held in between. It will be a kind of consolidation.

If the annual interview is held without any short-term progress interviews in between, clearly it will need more thorough preparation.

Some long-term interviews are imposed by an employer throughout the organization as an attempt to remedy bad management. If staff work for years without ever being told whether they are doing a good or a bad job, their morale and efficiency will suffer. People have as much need of, and more right to, recognition, servicing, and repair, as the machines they operate. But the right kind of interview is not necessarily the same across the board. There has to be a compromise between forcing all managers into a centrally-designed strait-jacket which will make a number of people most uncomfortable, and on the other hand giving each manager so much room for manoeuvre that he can continue to avoid interviewing his subordinates altogether. This needs tackling from a number of different directions at once. Training, starting progress interviews at the top and working down, writing the Job Descriptions of senior managers so as to include some progress interviewing, and a gentle analysis of the problems in the more difficult areas, can all contribute to a solution.

9   *JOB OBJECTIVES*

An employee is entitled to know what standard of work is expected of him. One purpose in having a written set of Job Objectives for each job is simply to tell him that standard.

The second, related purpose is to prevent the progress interview, and other interviews, from being merely an exchange of impressions and opinions. A good worker is one who gets good results; not the one with an attractive personality or an aggressive voice, unless these go with good results.

Job Objectives should be based on the Job Description (see p. 28). They should highlight those duties which contribute most to success or failure. Against each duty should be given an Objective of quantity or quality. A typist might have a Job Objective giving the number of pages, or square inches, of typing an hour, and a maximum number of complaints or errors a week.

Job Objectives, whether of quantity or quality (and the two overlap) should as far as possible be matters of fact, admitting no dispute. If the Objectives have to be matters of judgment, the judge should be someone other than the boss or subordinate.

Those who are accustomed to vague qualities of the kind sometimes mentioned on Assessment Forms, as 'initiative', 'good influence', and 'technical knowledge', will not see how to translate these into Job Objectives. Indeed, as long as they remain simply words which one man attributes to another, it cannot be done. If employees are employed and paid simply for characteristics they possess, and not for any work they might do, there is no place for Job Objectives, nor for progress interviews either. And no doubt there are such people, from the Director who is employed because he is a peer, to the receptionist who is employed for having large breasts. But wherever it is possible to say that there is a job to do, it is also possible to say whether it is being done well or badly. There is an 'acceptable standard' of results, the 'end' to which human qualities are merely 'means'. It is these results which must be written into the Job Objectives.

The Job Objectives of a manager include the Job Objectives of all his subordinates, to be achieved through them. If there is a failure, both have failed, and must discuss the reasons and overcome the failure together.

If the Job Objectives are all known, and precisely measured, the subordinate may know how he is doing without being told. The interview in his case will summarise this knowledge, taking a bird's-eye view; discuss the reasons for any unexpected or significant results; and plan the future. But in many cases the subordinate will not know how he is doing, until he is told, because some of the relevant facts or judgements are available first to his boss.

10 PREPARATION

The most important and difficult part of the preparation is to establish how much ground one interview can usefully cover; and, given that time and nervous energy are limited, what to include and what to leave out. Let this decision establish the 'scope' of the interview.

Many authorities hold that it is unwise to discuss salary, or promotion, or to set targets or objectives for the future, in the progress interview. These matters take so much time and energy that other points will be crowded out. At the same time, the subordinate will often feel that these matters are a natural 'follow-up' from a discussion about progress. The boss must therefore decide in advance of the interview what he is to do. If they are to be excluded from this interview, when are they to be discussed? He must be able to explain at the beginning of the progress interview what matters are ruled out and why, and refer these matters to a later occasion.

The subordinate needs to prepare too and he may need help in this. Many employers invite the subordinate to put down in writing, perhaps on an official form, their own interests, difficulties, needs, successes, ambitions, questions, and suggestions. Further, it may be useful for either boss or subordinate to suggest one or two items for the agenda of the actual interview, a week or two before the interview happens. Both can then think about these items in advance.

11   *STRUCTURE*

The structure, or sequence, of the progress interview will again depend on what it is to include, and which of the aims it will serve. It is worthy emphasising that there is no one universally correct type of progress interview; but whatever the type, the interviewer must define the purpose and outline the scope and limits of the interview early on.

There is however one problem common to most interviews. If there are good points and bad, which should come first? The natural inclination of the interviewer is to take the good points first. They're least 'troublesome' (though they can cause trouble, when the subordinate disagrees with the boss on their importance). They give the boss time to get on the subordinate's wavelength and win his confidence. They help to put the subordinate at ease.

Against this method there are two arguments:

1 The subordinate will be reserving his attention mainly for anything critical. If all the good points come first, he may not be thinking about them, but be working out what the criticisms are

2 It is important to end on a 'good' note

The best answer may well be to have a careful and, if necessary, long introduction to the interview. This should not only describe the purposes and scope, as already indicated, but give the structure of the interview, indicating that the strengths of the subordinate will be discussed after his weaknesses. Moreover, the introduction should include some reassurance that the overall assessment is satisfactory. Normally either the performance and results are, broadly, satisfactory, or they are unsatisfactory and the structure of the reprimand interview is more appropriate. Where there is a firmly square peg in an unchangeable round hole, neither satisfaction nor reprimand are in order. Something has gone wrong with the selection procedure. It will probably be important to emphasise that the mistake is not the fault of the victim, and in his interests as well as the employer's, we must find him a more suitable job. Such an introduction should lead on naturally to a constructive interview.

Planning a careful structure is vital in this interview; the temptation to disgress is powerful, and sometimes a digression is a valuable way of relaxing, of standing back from the interview, of renewing strength before the next problem. But the boss must know that he is digressing, and be able to bring the conversation back. There is nothing like an intermediate summing up for this purpose.

12   *CONCLUSION*

The progress interview takes different forms, all of them
difficult. It represents in highly concentrated form the whole
art of management. If it succeeds, it is a powerful way of
leading, managing, and serving an individual subordinate. It
has many drawbacks and pitfulls, and can easily fail.

For the interview, manager and subordinate have to leave
their social relationship and concentrate on the work, and the
way work brings them together and separates them. But this
change of relationship, of 'hats', may have to be done slowly,
carefully, so that the subordinate is not given a jolt, and so
that the social relationship is preserved whatever happens in
the interview.

All emotion should be drained away. The 'putting at ease'
must include an attempt to assess how much fear and anger
there may be in the mind of the subordinate. Such emotions
have to be allayed, or harnessed to the purposes of the
interview, or they will obstruct these purposes. If they are
brought into the open early on, and the subordinate is allowed
to have his say at length, it is more likely that the progress
interview proper will go forward rationally. Where the
problems are too severe, or complicated, to be merely part of
the 'putting at ease' process, probably the progress interview
will have to be postponed, and a grievance interview held
instead.

Many of the problems and drawbacks can be overcome by
basing the interview on the subordinate, giving him the
initiative, and encouraging him to talk about difficulties and
successes. All of us do judge ourselves continually, though
often incorrectly, so the only skill involved is in persuading
the subordinate to think out loud. He will not tell the whole

truth of his assessment; who ever tells the whole truth in the presence of his boss? And the boss should not expect him to. But if the interview is successful, it should benefit the subordinate. It may as well start from his point of view.

Progress interviews which are compulsory, by order of the employer, start at a disadvantage. 'Well, my man, you will no doubt have heard on the grapevine that we all have to discuss and appraise the progress of each subordinate at this interview.' The work situation itself should be enough justification for some kind of a progress interview, but the kind of interview which the work requires may not accord with the employer's legislation. Occasionally a special interview might not seem to serve any purpose, and if neither boss nor subordinate can see any point, it is better not to hold the interview.

A manager cannot do his job well if he cannot conduct progress interviews, any more than if he cannot give orders or keep discipline. A good manager starts with some native wit in interviewing, reinforced by training and classroom practice in giving progress interviews, and before each interview does his preparation thoroughly.

13   SUMMARY NOTES

Aims

1 To improve individual performance by recognition and guidance
2 To reconcile the man's own ambitions with the employer's objectives

The progress interview

Preparation

1 Study the Job Objectives
2 Analyse the achievement of each Objective
3 Consider the man's potential; whether he is being fully 'stretched'; what changes could be made so that the job would use his full capacity
4 Consider the forms of recognition and reward open to him, apart from private congratulation at the interview:
   a financial
   b promotion
   c privileges
   d extra responsibility or assistance
   e training
5 Plan the progress interview in relation to his long-term development, and the development of the organisation
6 Avoid holding the interview at a time of crisis
7 Give the man at least a week's notice of the forthcoming interview, and invite him to prepare for it

Structure

1 Put at ease
2 State the nature of the interview
3 Give an overall impression of his work and progress
4 Outline the structure of the interview
5 Get understanding of the purpose of the interview
6 Get agreement on the main Job Objectives, and the achievement of each Objective
7 Discuss where improvement is possible, and how. Training?
8 Discuss strengths, and points for congratulation
9 Discuss his ambitions and enthusiasms
10 Any questions?
11 Sum up (in a job-centred and impersonal way)

12 Get agreement on Job Objectives for the next six to twelve months
13 Arrange the date of the next progress interview
14 End on a note of confidence, trust, and satisfaction

Check results

1 Watch the points raised for improvement, and congratulate if appropriate
2 Check performance in the job generally
3 Check relations and attitude
4 Prepare for the next progress interview

Chapter Five Role-Plays

1 *HOW TO ROLE-PLAY*

1 The roles marked *a* are for the boss or 'chairman', who should control the progress of the interview. The interview is held at his request, except in the cases of grievance interviews, which are at *b*'s request.

2 The tutor gives a role to each player. Players do not know what is in their opposite number's role. Sometimes it is helpful to give both players the same information, or to allow them to exchange information before the role-play begins. But separate roles are usually better, as the interviewer is forced to probe for information, and deal with unexpected twists in the dialogue.

3 Players are free to invent what facts they like, compatible with their own role. In theory their inventions might be incompatible with each other, leading to stalemate; but this seldom happens.

4 Remember the purpose of these role-plays is to practise the principles described, not to show off. Players and observers usually learn more from an interview that fails than from one that succeeds.

5 Players always want more information than they receive. The more information, the more life-like the role seems. But several pages take a long time to read and are difficult to remember, and the realism is even then an illusion. Tutors should settle for the briefest role that will allow the player to practise what he has learnt.

6 If the tutor can re-write these skeleton roles using terms and situations familiar to the players, they will be more successful. All roles are written for men, but any could be played by a woman with a few alterations to the wording.

7 Tape-recorders and closed circuit television are useful aids. They enable the tutor to re-play and analyse the interview in detail, and the participants to see the 'meaning' of pause, speed, tone, volume, position, gesture, etc. After the players have got over the first shock of hearing and seeing themselves as others do, the re-play will improve their performance and confidence.

8 Roles in selection and progress (appraisal) interviews may be played more thoroughly if time allows, using such records as application forms or assessment forms which the real situation requires.

9 It is good fun writing your own role-plays, but if the game is to be educational, make sure the roles illustrate at least one specific difficulty. On the other hand, avoid putting in too many teaching points, or none of them will emerge clearly. In my experience, the simplest role-play often yields the richest harvest of points for discussion.

2 SAMPLE ROLE-PLAYS

1*a* You have a personal assistant due to be transferred to Head Office in twelve months or so. You have a vacancy for a clerk at the moment. The successful clerk will have to work independently when you and the personal assistant are at Conferences; and at holiday times, and when there is sickness. You also want to make him responsible to the personal assistant, with a view to possibly succeeding the personal assistant in due course. Interview an applicant.

1*b* You are a candidate for a clerical vacancy. For the last two years you have had a boring routine job in the Invoicing Department as a junior clerk. You want a job with more initiative. You are 22 years old, with 5 'O' levels and one 'A' level (Geography). At school you were captain of the football team, and edited the school magazine. You are the oldest of four children. Do *not* volunteer any information.

2*a* Play the role of your present job. You have to welcome to your team a new employee, aged 18. He is said to be a recruit of promise, who deserves training and development. It is his first working day with your organization, and you have to tell him whatever he ought to know, or wants to know, on that day. He will report directly to you.

2*b* You are aged 18. You have joined this organization as a poor second-best to going to university (where you could not secure a place). You want to continue your education if possible in the new job, about which you know little in detail. You are shy and reluctant to talk in strange surroundings.

3*a* You are a manager in charge of several offices. In one the senior clerk, Wiggins, had a breakdown two months ago and went to hospital. It was uncertain if he would return. You are lucky to get the services of an efficient replacement, who runs his office superbly. Your own boss now tells you that Wiggins has recovered and will be back in a fortnight, and that the replacement will also be remaining with you. You decide to tell the replacement that Wiggins is returning.

3*b* You were brought in as office supervisor two months ago when your predecessor, Mr Wiggins, had a breakdown and went to hospital. The office works well and you enjoy it. No-one has told you whether Wiggins is to return, nor what happens to you if he does. The boss sends for you.

4*a* You are the supervisor of a punched-card installation. You have put an operator with experience of manual card punching on to an automatic tape-to-card punch. As he is new, you have been keeping an eye on him, and have just found him working with one connection loose. One batch of cards will need re-punching. Speak to him about it.

4*b* You work in a punched-card installation. After experience on a manual punch, you have just been put on to an automatic tape-to-card punch. It looked simple enough, but your supervisor has just come up to you and found a loose connection. Play the role as though you were flustered, annoyed with yourself, and annoyed with him if he should make any unjustified criticism.

Role-plays

5*a* You have been made head of a small section that keeps statistical records. The section is efficient and morale is high but timekeeping is poor. Last week a senior manager advised you not to let timekeeping get slack; it 'let the side down, and made it difficult for other managers to keep their staff up to the mark'. You decide to speak to a junior member of your staff who is practically never on time and who was 20 minutes late this morning (the hours are 9 am to 5 pm).

5*b* You are a junior member of a small and happy section that keeps statistical records. You have just passed your driving test and bought a car. You have joined a group of drivers who live near you and work at the same establishment, and take turns to drive each other in. One of the group is a senior scientist who is not much concerned with punctuality; this morning, for instance, he drove you in and you were 15 minutes late. The hours are 9 am to 5 pm. The section has recently got a new boss and you are afraid he may demand punctuality. The boss has sent for you.

6*a* You are the Safety Officer. You have gone into a workshop and found a man working a guillotine without putting the guard in position. You caught him doing this last week and warned him. He complained that the guard held up his work, but you pointed out that it was a Safety Regulation. You feel he must now be reprimanded.

6*b* The Safety Officer has found you in your workshop using the guillotine without the safety guard. He told you not to do this last week. But you resent the guard, which slows down the work and reduces your bonus. As the Safety Officer is not your boss, you need not take much notice; you can't work for two bosses, and your own foreman turns a blind eye.

86

7*a* You are a Personnel Manager. You have to conduct a progress interview with an Assistant Personnel Officer whose work has been reliable but unimaginative. He gets on well with his colleagues in the Department, and is a good influence. You might be able to find him a promotion next year, if he showed more enthusiasm for modern techniques of personnel management. He would also be well-advised to make himself better known to the staff, and to acquaint himself with their problems.

7*b* You are an Assistant Personnel Officer, due to have your progress interview. Your wife has been ill lately, and the burden of looking after her and your three children as well as the job has been difficult. You have not talked about it much because you do not think it is your employer's business. You know you have not shown much initiative at work, partly for fear of being given a lot of the extra documentation the organization now requires. But you want to give a good impression at the interview.

8*a* You are a Plant Manager, about to give a foreman his progress interview. Since he joined your organization five years ago his record was good, until lately. He has been unwilling to co-operate with the Work Study team going round the plant, and the team has hardly been able to obtain any accurate measurements of the work of his section. Other foremen are not so unreasonable, and you want to change his attitude to be more like theirs. Work Study is an important part of the management's plan to contain costs and keep competitive; they have given assurances that no one will lose their jobs as a result of Work Study.

8*b* You are a foreman, going for a progress interview with your Plant Manager. You have been worried by the Work Study team which has lately been trying to measure the work of your section. You were declared redundant from your last job five years ago after a similar Work Study campaign, and (despite management promises that no-one will lose their job) you think the campaign is intended to make the men work harder for less pay, and eventually reduce the number on the payroll. You have therefore advised your men to go slow when their work is being measured.

9*a* You are manager of an assembly plant for motor accessories. Yesterday you spent some time meeting shop stewards, discussing a possible new bonus incentive scheme. It has always been your policy to take the shop stewards into your confidence early on, and get them to put proposals to the shop floor; you think this saves time in the long run. But it has put you behind with your normal work. Your oldest foreman has asked to see you, and although you have a lot to do, you agree.

9*b* You are a foreman in an assembly plant. You have been angry for some time with your Plant Manager, who seems to tell everything to the shop stewards before he tells you. Today your steward is full of a new bonus incentive scheme that the manager discussed yesterday. To preserve your own authority your pretended to know something about it, and you ask to see the boss, to find out about the scheme, and to have a real row about the way you are kept in the dark.

10*a* You are the Works Manager. In the recent batch of promotions to foreman, one of your older workers has been passed by. This is the result of a new policy which replaces promotion according to seniority by promotion of those of higher technical education, and requires the promotion of younger men so that the organization can get longer service from them, and perhaps promote them higher. Your 'senior citizen' has asked to see you.

10*b* You are in your late 40s and were expecting to be promoted foreman on seniority. You have heard rumours of a new policy, but didn't realise what it meant until you were passed over in the latest batch of promotions. You are angry about this, since you can do any job in the shop better than any of the younger men. You have asked to see your Works Manager to see what is going on.

11*a* You are a storekeeper with two clerks working for you. One of them is on leave. The other one takes his lunch late, with your permission, and usually has sandwiches in the office. An engineer has come to see you with a complaint. Your staff tell you that this engineer asks for items of equipment which are not usually kept in stock, and when they are ordered for him he no longer requires them.

11*b* You are an engineer and have gone to the storekeeper to complain about the attitude of his staff. They are ignorant and unhelpful. Shortly after lunch you went to get some valves, and the man in the office was reading a paper. He said, 'Help yourself'. You couldn't find what you wanted, and he said 'Perhaps we're out of stock'.

12*a* You are head of a small information department. One of your best workers, a graduate of 24 who is good at abstracting, has suddenly given notice and you cannot discover why. You were away when he gave notice, but you are back in the department now, and he is leaving next week. You feel there is something wrong with the situation, and ask him in for a final chat.

12*b* You are a graduate of 24. You joined the organization six months ago, hoping for a progressive job. You are in a small information department, doing boring and routine work with no prospects. You have given notice and are leaving next week. Your boss, who was away when you gave notice, always tries to jolly you along instead of listening to your complaints. If he talks sympathetically to you at the interview, you could suggest that in future they treat graduates with respect, give them more responsibility (allow them to deal with outsiders without supervision, for example), talk to them about their progress and prospects, and welcome their suggestions. But don't bother saying all this unless he asks properly.

13*a* You are a manager responsible for the work of a commercial records section whose supervisor is leaving in a month's time. This supervisor has asked to see you. Part of the problem is no doubt tying up the job before he goes. Another problem might be Mr Gherkins, who shares the office and telephone. Mr Gherkins' job is to chase up supplies, so he spends a lot of time on the telephone. When he was transferred to you last month there was no proper office for him to go to, so you had to put him with the commercial records people.

13*b* You are the supervisor of a commercial records section, but leaving in a month's time. Most of the job you hand over to your successor will be straightforward, but a new man, Mr Gherkins, is a bit of a headache. He shares your room and telephone although he is not in your section. He spends most of the day on the telephone talking to suppliers, and affecting the concentration and morale of your section. You ask to see the manager to press him to find Mr Gherkins another place.

14*a* You are in charge of a research laboratory. You have had an assistant, aged 20, working for you for about six months. He does not seem stupid, but he has to be told what to do all the time. He has been ticked off twice for starting a process without completing the safety procedures, and twice for not getting on with the job. Talk to him about his progress.

14*b* You are a laboratory assistant aged 20. You have been working for your present boss for about six months. The section does not seem to be very busy and frequently you do not have enough to do. Your boss has twice spotted that you started a process before the safety procedures were complete, and has nagged you a couple of times about not working fast enough. You are worried about your gambling debts: you now owe about six months' salary to various friends, but your boss does not (you hope) know about this yet.

3   COMMENTS ON EACH ROLE-PLAY

1 The boss should not say anything which could be construed as promise of promotion. The applicant may not be suitable; the personal assistant's transfer may not come through. If a promise made at a selection interview is broken, you have an embittered employee on your hands.

2 At this interview bosses tend to talk too much and listen too little. New recruits take in little on their first day.

3 Before the interview the boss must take a firm decision, probably that Wiggins will be in charge when he returns, and communicate this unpleasant fact clearly in the interview.

4 As the operator is new, he needs explanation and encouragement, not anger, however annoying his mistake is.

Role-plays

5 The latecomer must agree with the boss on the facts of his lateness and his conditions of employment, and accept his duty to reconcile the two. If the boss can give him help or advice, so much the better. But the car, other late employees, the senior scientist, and the actual number of minutes late, are all 'red herrings'.

6 Only a man's superior can effectively reprimand him. The Safety Officer should know what sanctions (reporting etc.) are open to him.

7 The Personnel Manager should be able to uncover the home background. He may go on to inspire the Assistant to develop his interests; but if the home problems have spoiled the atmosphere for discussing the work, he should postpone discussion of the work to a later interview.

8 The Plant Manager should question the foreman to elicit the strength of his feelings. It may be worth admitting that the Work Study campaign has not been properly explained. The boss could suggest a meeting between the Work Study staff and all the foremen, to discuss how all can benefit from the campaign.

9 The manager should welcome this complaint, as a chance to correct an important and common failing: by-passing the foreman. He should discuss how to prevent it happening again, but this must be a managerial policy, not an abdication of power.

10 Management have not communicated a change in promotion policy, and the Works Manager is taking the consequences. Logically, the new policy should help the organization directly, and indirectly the man himself. But logic will not heal wounded pride; the interview is easier to conduct if the man can be found a·new job, well away from

those who know he has missed promotion. If the new job has an impressive title, so much the better.

11 The boss should not admit his subordinates have behaved badly before he has heard their side of the story.

12 This interview should give constructive feedback affecting selection policy (not recruiting people too well qualified for the job), the selection interview (warning recruits about a job's snags), and human relations after recruitment.

13 The boss should collect and record the facts; judge them; decide whether to confirm them (perhaps by staying for a time in the office); and if the problem is correctly stated, pass it to someone who can solve it.

14 If the gambling problem is not to interfere with the man's work, the boss must uncover it, question and listen with sympathy, and either pass it to a Personnel or Welfare officer, or deal with it himself. Objectively the problem is easy to cope with, once the frightened victim is not trying to sort it out by himself.

4   ROLE-PLAY CHECK LIST

The purpose of listening carefully to an interview and assessing its progress is to help the interviewer to recognize how it looks to an outsider, and so improve his own 'technique, and to provide the basis for discussing, analysing, and learning from the interview after it is over.

Discussion is much more fruitful if you attach your comments to specific words or phrases. Do not try to cover every point below; it is better to make a detailed observation on one or two.

Role-plays

1 *Opening*

Was the atmosphere created at the begining helpful?
Was the transition from greeting to business a smooth one?
Did the interviewee understand the kind of interview it was,
and its purpose?

2 *Structure*

Was the structure suitable for this interview?
Was the interview long enough?
Did the interviewer put his case clearly?
Did he keep control of the interview?
Did he ask for questions?
Did he listen enough?
Did he sum up after each main point, and at the end?

3 *Style*

Were the words well-chosen for this particular interviewee?
Was the interviewer sincere? Was he friendly and polite?
Did he keep control of himself?
Was the degree of participation satisfactory?
Were relationships good for the purposes of the interview?

4 *Ending*

Was the interview well summarized?
Were differences of opinion fairly treated?
Did the parties agree on a conclusion?
Was it clear what was to happen next?
Was the agreed conclusion and action tied in to the purpose
of the interview, as stated at the opening?
Was the interview good 'public relations' for management?
What, of permanent value, did the interview achieve?

94

INDEX